IMAGES
of America

BOEING

W.E. Boeing (right) and Eddie Hubbard in March 1919 in front of the C-700 seaplane at Vancouver, Canada. The C-700 was used by William Boeing to carry the first US international contract airmail from Seattle to British Columbia.

IMAGES
of America

BOEING

Compiled by
Martin W. Bowman

TEMPUS

Tempus Publishing Limited
The Mill, Brimscombe Port,
Stroud, Gloucestershire, GL5 2QG

ISBN 0 7524 1537 9

Typesetting and origination by
Tempus Publishing Limited
Printed in Great Britain by
Midway Clark Printing, Wiltshire

After the war, Boeing capitalized on their wartime production successes by producing many notable civil and military designs, such as the C-135 series, which was also the progenitor of the Model 707 transports, and the B-52 Stratofortress nuclear bomber, which was the backbone of Strategic Air Command from June 1965 until the early 1990s.

Contents

The main building (known as the 'Red Barn') at the former Heath Shipyard, a small yacht-building firm on the Duwamish River, which Boeing used from 1917 It is seen here on 8 June 1917 when it was under guard. The Red Barn was restored in the 1970s and re-located to Boeing Field as part of the Museum of Flight complex.

Acknowledgements

The author would like to thank: Mike Bailey; Tom Lubbesmeyer of the Boeing Co.; Kenneth Fields; Wallace Fields; Tom Fitton; Brian Foskett; Lt-Col. Harry D. Gobrecht; Terry Holloway; Marshall Aerospace; Brian McGuire; Jerry C. Scutts; Hans Heri Stapfer; Graham M. Simons; the dedicated staff of the US 2nd Air Division Memorial Library in Norwich, including Derek S. Hills, Trust Librarian; Linda J. Berube, American Fulbright Librarian; Lesley Fleetwood; and Christine Snowden – all of whom were most helpful and who provided much willing assistance with research.

Introduction

The Boeing Company was founded by William E. Boeing, the son of a wealthy timberman. At the age of thirty-four, Boeing took up flying for his own amusement. After a couple of rides, he became convinced that he could build a better aeroplane. He and Commander G. Conrad Westervelt, a Navy officer assigned to engineering work at a shipyard in Seattle, Washington, decided to build a pair of seaplanes. By December 1915, an aeroplane called the 'B & W Seaplane' was under construction in a hangar on the east shore of Lake Union. *Bluebird*, the first B & W, was completed in early 1916, marking the modest beginning of aircraft production at the Boeing Company. It flew for the first time on 29 June 1916.

Although aircraft work had been in progress since 1915, corporate identity was not achieved until the Pacific Aero Products Company was incorporated on 15 July 1916. On 26 April 1917 the name was changed to The Boeing Airplane Company, without change of corporate structure or management. The small speciality shop, with a twenty-one-man workforce, became a major aircraft manufacturer during the First World War. The Model C followed the B & W and was the first all-Boeing design. The US Navy ordered two Model Cs for testing. US entry into the First World War created a sudden demand for primary training planes. As a result, fifty additional Model Cs were ordered. Later, one additional Model C was built for William E. Boeing. This was logically called the C-700 because the previous airframe had been known in the shops by its US Navy serial number, 699. The C-700 was used by William Boeing and Eddie Hubbard to carry the first US international contract airmail from Seattle to British Columbia (see page 2). In 1918 Boeing was asked to build fifty Curtiss HS-2L flying boats for the US Navy.

The Boeing Company, which had moved its manufacturing facilities to the

The Boeing aeroplane factory, 1 December 1928. A few of the original Heath Shipyard buildings can be seen behind the large assembly plant at the water's edge.

In 1921, Boeing won a contract to build 200 Thomas-Morse MB-3A pursuit planes for the AAC. It provided the company with valuable design experience that enabled Boeing to build a successful series of pursuit aircraft between 1924 and 1936.

In the summer of 1928, the Model 83 (XF4B-1 No. 1) and the Model 89 (XF4B-1 No. 2, pictured here on 25 July 1928) flew for the first time. They led to very large P-12/F-4B production runs for the Army and the Navy respectively which by February 1933 totalled 586 aircraft.

Heath Shipyard on the Duwamish River, south of Seattle, struggled through the first disastrous post-war years by accepting military orders for the manufacture of Sea Sled boats, canoes, and bedroom furniture. Not until 1920 did prospects look better, when the production of 200 Thomas Morse MB-3A single-seat fighters and rebuilding of 354 Liberty-engined de Havilland DH-4s was undertaken from 1920 to 1925. The early fame of Boeing was earned by its position as the leading supplier of single-seat fighting planes between 1924 and 1936. Work on the Boeing Model 15 biplane fighter began in 1922 and the XPW-9 flew for the first time on 2 June 1923. Forty-nine PW-9 production models for the Army followed. Ten FB-1 models were ordered by the Navy. Further improvements kept the Model 15 in production until 1928, and improved versions and new models continued into the late 1930s.

In 1929, ninety examples of the Boeing P-12B were ordered, the largest single Army order for fighters since 1921. Altogether, 586 aircraft in the P-12/F-4B series were delivered to the Army and the Navy (and a few overseas); the last was on 28 February 1933. Boeing's Model 248, which appeared in March 1932, was the first all-metal monoplane fighter and three prototypes were built at its own expense. After testing as the XP-936, the Army purchased these and went on to order 136 P-26 production examples.

Before the fighter business tapered off, Boeing switched production to the potentially more lucrative transport business. When transcontinental airmail routes operated by the Post Office Department were handed over to private operators in 1927, Boeing's low bid for the key leg from San Francisco to Chicago was accepted and a new airline subsidiary, Boeing Air Transport, was formed. The Seattle factory redesigned their 1925 Model 40 to take the new air-cooled Wasp engine and built twenty-four Model 40As in just six months, ready for service with the new airline. Its competitors, meanwhile, continued to use the heavier, water-cooled, Liberty-engined aircraft for mail service. In addition to having space for 1,200lb of air mail, the Model 40A had room for two passengers in a small cabin ahead of the pilot's open cockpit. Later models carried four passengers. A total of eighty-two Model 40s were built. Their introduction signalled the beginning of regular commercial passenger services over long distances and served as the vehicle for the first regular passenger and night mail flights.

The success of the passenger operations with Model 40s on the San Francisco-Chicago route encouraged expansion of the business through the addition of larger aircraft designed specifically for passenger convenience and comfort. In 1928 Pacific Air Transport (PAT), a San Francisco to Seattle airline, was purchased. The two airlines were merged to become The Boeing System. The first of four Model 80 tri-motor biplanes, the last word in air transportation, was delivered to Boeing Air Transport in August 1928, only two weeks after its first flight. Twelve passengers and later eighteen passengers were carried in a large cabin provided with hot and cold running water, a toilet, forced air ventilation, leather upholstered seats and individual reading lamps. The needs of a dozen or more passengers during long flights soon indicated the desirability of a cabin attendant who could devote full attention to their comfort. While some European airlines used male stewards, Boeing Air Transport hired female registered nurses who became the first of the now-universal stewardesses. The pilot and co-pilot were enclosed in a roomy cabin ahead of and separate from the passenger cabin.

Boeing, meanwhile, expanded rapidly. In February 1929 it acquired the Hamilton Metalplane Co. of Milwaukee, Wisconsin, and that summer established a Canadian subsidiary (Boeing Aircraft of Canada) in Vancouver, Canada, where it began building C-204 flying boats. A powerful holding company was formed with the merger of the Boeing aeroplane and airline operations and Pratt & Whitney, a leading aeroplane engine manufacturer, Hamilton Aero Manufacturing Co., and another aeroplane manufacturer, Chance Vought Corporation, to form the United Aircraft and Transport Corporation. Each company continued to produce its own specialized product under its own name while the airlines operated under their own names within a holding company known as United Air Lines. Three airlines were acquired and added to the existing operation, while the manufacturing companies Sikorsky Aviation and Standard Steel Propeller Co. were bought up.

With one eye on the military trainer market, on 1 April 1938 the Boeing Aircraft Company bought the Stearman Aircraft Co., based in Wichita, Kansas, to create the Stearman Aircraft Division (renamed the Wichita Division in 1941). Beginning in 1939, the Wichita plant began turning out Stearman primary biplane trainers by the hundred for the US Navy and US

Boeing Wichita, Kansas, built and owned by the US government for B-29 production, turned out 1,644 Superfortresses. The original Stearman Aircraft Co. buildings (Plant 1) can be seen in the background.

Army Air Corps. Stearmans were destined to be built in greater numbers than any other biplane in American history.

When markets for new aeroplane designs developed, Boeing was ready with new models and processes. It was the first American manufacturer to use welded steel tubing for fuselage structure, a feature that soon became standard throughout the industry until generally replaced by monocoque sheet metal structures in the mid-1930s. Boeing again demonstrated its technological leadership by introducing this new construction, matched to aerodynamically advanced aeroplanes, in both commercial and military production with the Monomail, B-9 and 247 models of 1930-33.

The all-metal Model 200 Monomail mail and cargo carrier, which first flew on 6 May 1930, was one of the most revolutionary aeroplanes in commercial aviation history. Designed initially as a combination mail and passenger aeroplane, its increased performance resulted from structural and aerodynamic refinements, not the addition of brute horsepower. The traditional biplane design with drag-producing struts and wires was replaced by a single, smooth, all-metal low wing of clean cantilever construction. The wheels were retracted into the wing during flight, and the drag of the air-cooled Hornet engine was

During the 1930s Boeing also produced some exciting transport and bomber aircraft. The Model 214 (Y1B-9) of 1931 was a military development of the Monomail mail and cargo carrying plane.

greatly reduced by enclosing it in a newly developed anti-drag cowling. However, the Monomail's sleek aerodynamic design was too advanced for the power plants of the day. Efficient use of its full performance range required a variable-pitch propeller. When one was eventually installed, the aircraft was already on the verge of being replaced by the newer multi-engine designs it had inspired.

Boeing Models 214 and 215, which became the US Army Y1B-9 and YB-9,

The P-26A (Model 248) was the first all-metal monoplane in Air Corps pursuit-squadron service and 136 'Peashooters' were delivered between 1933 and 1936.

Ever innovative, Boeing cleaned up the P-36 design to produce, in 1934, the XP-940 pursuit monoplane, but the gross weight restricted manoeuvrability and service ceiling and P-29A production orders never materialized. Boeing dropped out of the fighter business and concentrated instead on bombers.

were logical military developments of the Monomail. Boeing embarked on the two B-9 projects as a private venture in anticipation that they would produce the same performance advance in the area of heavy bombers as the Monomail had done in the commercial sector, but the type was not ordered in quantity. The B-9 did, however, prove a major advance in bomber design and it greatly influenced the Model 247, the first airliner produced in quantity by Boeing.

An unprecedented decision was made to re-equip completely the Boeing Air Transport System with the innovative new twelve-seater transport and an order for sixty Model 247s was placed while the design was still in the mock-up stage. The Model 247 was the first all-metal streamlined monoplane transport. It was powered by two supercharged Pratt and Whitney 550hp S1D1 Wasps (the first time superchargers had been used on a transport type) and featured retractable landing gear, an enclosed cabin, auto pilot, trim tabs, and de-icing equipment.

In 1934 Congress passed legislation which forced aircraft and engine manufacturers to end all their links with airline operations. On 26 September, a government trust-busting suit, which divorced aeroplane and engine manufacturers from airline operations, had separated United Aircraft's airline and manufacturing activities and the Boeing Aircraft Company, renamed from the Boeing Airplane Company and a separate entity from Boeing Air Transport, had pulled out of United. The Boeing Aircraft Company resumed independent operation and moved into the bomber business.

In the 1930s it was accepted that a formation of unescorted bombers could

Flown for the first time on 28 July 1935 by the company test pilot Leslie Tower, the Model 299 signalled the beginning of the long line of famous Flying Fortress models for the USAF in the Second World War.

get through to their target if they were properly arranged and adequately armed. During air manoeuvres in 1933 pursuits repeatedly failed to intercept the bombers and there was even talk of eliminating pursuits altogether. Funds for new aircraft were very limited and it was mostly manufacturers who funded new developments which in turn might attract orders from the military. (By 1934, Model 247 production was winding down and the only business Boeing had was unfinished contracts for P-26A and C fighters. In August, 1,100 of its 1,700 workforce were laid off. Cash in hand was barely $500,000.)

Boeing's first bomber development, in 1934, was the massive Model 294, or the XBLR-1 (experimental bomber, long range), which became the XB-15. That same year the Air Corps issued a specification for a 'multi-engined' bomber, but manufacturers would have to build prototypes at their own expense. Although the term 'multi-engined' generally meant two engines, the four-engined Model 299 was already in the design stage and so, on 16 September 1934, Boeing boldly decided to invest $275,000 in the Model 299. (Ultimately, it would cost over $432,000 to build a prototype.) The new design, which was to become famous as the B-17, incorporated many lessons learned with the X-15, B-9 and Model 247. Powered by four 750hp Pratt and Whitney Hornet radials, it would carry all bombs internally and accommodate a crew of eight.

Completed in only a year, the Model 299 was rolled out at Boeing Field on 17

In the Second World War Boeing turned out 2,300 B-17Fs (42-30243 from Block B-17F-95-BO is pictured). The F was followed by 4,035 Boeing-built 'G' models for the war effort.

July 1935. A *Seattle Times* reporter dubbed the fifteen-ton machine – to be used in a defensive role to protect the American coastline from enemy surface fleets – a 'flying fortress'. At first, testing went very well indeed, but on 30 October 1935 the Model 299 crashed and burst into flames, killing Leslie Tower, the test pilot, and Major 'Pete' Hill, AAC. An investigation concluded that the crash was a result of the mechanical ground locks not having been unlocked prior to take off. This prevented movement of the main surfaces. This setback cost Boeing dearly. On 17 January 1936, Douglas received an order for 133 B-18s, while Boeing received only a service test order for thirteen improved B-299Bs and a static test model.

The first Y1B-17 also crashed, on 7 December 1936, but pilot error was to blame. The thirteen service test Y1B-17s went into service with the AAC and established many long-distance records, earning a well deserved reputation for rugged construction and reliable operation. Further production orders were slow – a requirement for just ten B-17Bs was received in August 1937, and only twenty-nine more by June 1938. The Government strained relations further by haggling over the cost of each bomber. Boeing was a small, independent company, with barely 600 employees, and tooling up in anticipation of large production orders had left them with no cash reserves. Eventually, the Army

A new government-owned plant at Renton built 1,122 B-29A-BN Superfortresses by May 1946. At the end of the war the Renton and Wichita plants closed. Increased demand for military transports, however, led to the reopening of the Renton plant for the manufacture of C-97s in 1949, while Wichita re-opened for the conversion of B-29 tankers. Renton then took over this contract when Wichita was used to build B-47s and it subsequently went on to produce Boeing 135s and a succession of commercial jet transports.

agreed to pay $202,500 per B-17 – little consolation given the myriad problems which frequently arose with armament, navigational and bombing apparatus and engines, especially superchargers, which were a radical innovation at this time.

B-17B models were delivered to the AAC in 1939-40. Fitted with the Norden bomb sight for precision bombing, they soon gained a reputation for accuracy: it was said that a B-17 was able, in daylight, to drop a bomb in a 'pickle barrel' from 20,000ft! Pioneering operations in Europe by the RAF, which purchased twenty Fortress Is, soon exploded this myth. Combat experience was to reveal other deficiencies, notably armament, which were only alleviated by installing power-operated gun turrets. Bombing results were little better from 1942 onwards when the B-17 largely equipped the US 8th Air Force in East Anglia. As enemy defences improved, more and more guns were added, and the Fort got heavier and heavier. Losses on occasion were critical yet, largely due to the introduction of long-range escort fighters, the Fortress remained in production throughout the Second World War, serving in every theatre. When production finished, a staggering 12,731 B-17s had been built by

In August 1952 Boeing announced plans to invest $16 million to build an entirely new jet-powered transport, the Model 707. The prototype was followed, from 12 January 1958 onwards, by 725 commercial examples.

Boeing, Douglas and Lockheed. Of these, Boeing produced 6,981.

Another war-winning bomber to emerge from the Second World War was Boeing's even bigger B-29 Superfortress, which had been conceived as far back as 1938. Its fuselage was divided into three pressurized compartments, two of which were connected by a tunnel over the tandem bomb bays. It was far ahead of its contemporaries with ten-gun defensive armament in four remotely controlled power turrets and a single directly controlled tail turret. The first YB-29s were delivered to the 58th Very Heavy Bombardment Wing in July 1943. By the end of the year it was decided that the B-29 would equip the newly formed 20th Bomber Command in India and China for raids on Japanese targets. The first B-29 mission occurred on 5 June 1944. Throughout late 1944 and early 1945 the B-29s carried out high level daylight raids on Japanese targets, until in March 1945 Major General Curtis E. LeMay decided that as the B-29s could not hit their targets accurately, they must area bomb using incendiaries to burn up large areas of Japanese towns and cities in an attempt to wreck the Japanese war effort. All Japan came to fear the dreaded 'Bni-Ju's. In August 1945 two B-29s effectively brought the Pacific war to a dramatic and welcome end when atomic devices were dropped on Hiroshima and Nagasaki.

Altogether, 3,970 B-29s had been built when production ceased in 1946, including 2,766 by Boeing. In 1947 the improved B-50 Superfortress appeared, and that same year, on 17 December, the B-47 Stratojet pure jet bomber flew for the first time. In appearance, Boeing's final foray into the super-bomber business, the B-52 Stratofortress, was a direct development of the B-47. Designed as a nuclear bomber for service with SAC, the B-52 first flew on 15 April 1952, and altogether 744 B-52s were built, including 467 at Wichita.

Boeing meanwhile had also re-entered the commercial airliner market, starting in 1947 with the Model 377 Stratocruiser, which was produced side-by-side with B-50s on the Seattle production lines until 1949. Three years later, in August 1952, Boeing announced that it was investing $16 million of its own money to build the prototype of an entirely new jet-powered transport, the 367-80, or 707 prototype. The American jet transport era began when the 367-80 first flew on 15 July 1954. From then on Boeing made the long haul and short-to-medium-range markets their own, with a succession of hugely successful air transports, from the 707-120, -320, and -420 intercontinental airliners, through to the 727-100 and -200 series, and, in 1967, the 737.

If the introduction of the 707 had been innovative, the appearance of the gigantic 747 in February 1969 was revolutionary. Three years earlier, Pan Am had placed an order for twenty-five 747-100s, or 'jumbo jets' as the press quickly dubbed these behemoths which carried 500 passengers. A new 780-acre site had to be built before production could begin in early 1967. This included the world's largest building, the 200 million-cubic foot Everett plant, at Paine Field, thirty miles north of Seattle. On 30 September 1968, the first 747 was rolled out. By 1975, the 747 was being produced in seven different models. The 747-200 series was followed in the summer of 1980 by the 747-300 programme when Swiss Air ordered five aircraft. On 22 October 1985, Northwest Airlines were the first to order the even bigger 747-400 series.

Boeing's dominance in the commercial aircraft sector was further enhanced with the introduction of the 757 twinjet, which first flew in February 1982, and the 767 wide body twinjet, which entered commercial service on 8 September 1982. It is only now that this dominance has been seriously challenged by other manufacturers, such as Airbus. The 777, the newest member of the Boeing family, fits the same category as the McDonnell Douglas MD-11 and the Airbus A330/A340. On 29 October 1990, United Airlines placed a firm order for thirty-four 777 aircraft, plus an option for a further thirty-four. The 777 has effectively filled the capacity gap in that it can carry 375 to 400 passengers in two classes (the 767 carries between 290 and 325 passengers, while the newest 747 carries up to 566). With so many models to chose from it is not surprising therefore that the PR phrase 'If it's not Boeing, we're not going' was coined!

One
Diversity through Adversity

The XBLR-1 (XB-15) which flew on 15 October 1937 was a massive four-engined bomber which took three years to build, weighed over thirty-five tons, and was almost 88ft long. It had a 149ft span and passageways were built inside the wing to enable the crew to make minor repairs to the four Pratt & Whitney R-1830-11 engines while the aircraft was in flight. Armed with six machine guns, it contained complete living and sleeping quarters with sound-proofed, heated and ventilated cabins.

One of the two B & W twin-float sport seaplanes of 1916 – Boeing's first aircraft. The original factory was a boathouse on Seattle's Lake Union. The aircraft workers were skilled carpenters, shipwrights, cabinet makers, and seamstresses. The materials used were fine Washington State spruce lumber, steel wire, and linen fabric.

The Model 3 ('C' Series, C-4, 5, 6, 11) followed the B & W 1A and was the first 'all-Boeing' design. The US Navy ordered two Model Cs (5 and 6) for test from the Pacific Aero Products Co., which became the Boeing Airplane Company on 26 April 1917. Fifty additional Cs were ordered as US entry into the First World War created a sudden demand for primary training planes. Pictured in the boathouse on Seattle's Lake Union is the C-5, with clear-doped finish just prior to the new 1917 military tail striping being added. In the background is Mr Boeing's original Martin seaplane in the process of conversion to a land plane.

Fifty Model 5s (C-650-700, C-1F, CL4S), powered by a 100hp Hall-Scott A-7A, were ordered by the US Navy as primary trainers and these were serial numbered 650-699. A-650 is pictured in the boathouse on Lake Union on 22 April 1918.

Although not a Boeing design, the single 360hp Liberty-engined Curtiss HS-2L patrol flying boat, fifty of which were built by Boeing, significantly contributed to production experience and added to the incentive to design the first post-war Boeing aeroplane, the B-1 flying boat.

1B-1 (Model 6) flying boat was the first Boeing aeroplane designed from scratch as a practical commercial vehicle, and it first flew on 27 December 1919. Used continuously for eight years on the Seattle-Victoria airmail route, this single example was registered five times. N-ABNA was used from 1923-1927.

Single prototypes of the BB-1 (Model 7 – pictured), a smaller development of the B-1 which flew on 7 January 1920, and the BB-L6 (Model 8), a land plane using the same wings as the BB-1, were built but, like the B-1, never went into wider production, largely because of the flood of war-surplus machines which were available during the early 1920s.

After the First World War, Boeing subsisted mainly by modernizing existing military biplanes. In 1920, Boeing rebuilt 111 wooden de Havilland 1916 design DH4 'Liberty Planes' as DH-4B. From 1923 to 1925, 183 of the British two-seat day bombers were rebuilt with Boeing-designed steel tube fuselages as DH-4M-1 (for 'modernized'). Thirty of these were delivered to the US Marine Corps under the naval designation O2B-1, one went to the US Post Office, and six were delivered to Cuba.

In 1924 Boeing responded to an AAC request to design and build new wings for three DH-4M-1s in an attempt to extend the useful life of the aircraft. The new Model 42 that resulted was called the XCO-7 (Experimental Corps Observation, design No. 7). The XCO-7A was powered by a Liberty engine.

The XCO-7B (pictured) differed from the XCO-7A in that it was powered by an Army experimental inverted Liberty engine, and it had balanced elevators. The Model 42 did not enter full-scale production.

It was not until 1927-28, when war-surplus machine types had all but disappeared and commercial aviation was benefiting from the 'Lindbergh boom', that new types appeared. Two were the advanced versions of the B-1, known as the Model 6D (B1-D, pictured) and Model 6E (B1-E). The first of two B-1Ds flew in April 1928 and the first of six B-1Es flew on 4 March 1928.

In 1929 subsequent production B-1Es were designated Model 204s because of the great design advances made since 1919. One was built, a second was completed as a dual-control 204A for William E. Boeing, the third was completed by a private owner, and four C-204 'Thunderbirds' were built by Boeing-Canada (including *Pintail*, belonging to Western Canada Airways Ltd, pictured).

Ten armoured GA-1 ground attack triplanes powered by two 435hp Liberty 12A engines were built under an early post-war policy whereby the Army designed aeroplanes to its own requirements and then contracted out their manufacture by the aviation industry under competitive bidding. Although not a Boeing design, the GA-1, overweight and unpopular with cadets, which first flew in May 1921, was designated the Model 10.

Two GA-2 biplane prototypes powered by an untried single 750hp Engineering Division W-18 engine were built by Boeing. Since the new engine was unavailable at the time of the contract, a wooden mock-up was delivered!

The Model 50 (PB-1) (P for 'patrol') built in 1925 resulted from a 1924 US Navy requirement for a flying boat capable of flying 2,400 miles from California to Hawaii non-stop. The construction material was primarily metal, although the upper portion of the hull (pictured) was of laminated wood frames covered with wood veneer, and the wing and tail covering was fabric.

The PB-1 designation was changed to XPB-2 (pictured) when the Navy removed the tandem 800hp Packard 2A-2500 water-cooled engines and installed experimental Pratt & Whitney R-1860 Hornet air-cooled radials of 800hp. The PB-1 could carry 2,000lb of bombs or depth charges and various machine guns.

Three all-metal Model 63 aircraft (designated TB-1, T for 'torpedo', although the aircraft also doubled as a scout) were designed and built to US Navy specifications in 1927. These were powered by a 730hp Packard 3A-2500 and could be fitted out either as land planes for operation from carriers (the wings folded as a shipboard space-saving measure) or as twin-pontoon seaplanes. A-7024 (pictured), the first TB-1, flew on 4 May 1927.

27

The Model 40 was built for a 1925 US Post Office Department competition to find a replacement for the converted military de Havilland 4s that had carried the airmail since 1918. The Government purchased '775' (pictured), the single Model 40, but Boeing received no production contract. The Model 40A was revived in 1926 when indications were that the transcontinental mail routes would be turned over to private operators in 1927. The war-surplus water-cooled 400hp Liberty engine was replaced on the newly built aircraft by the 420hp Pratt & Whitney Wasp, a new air-cooled radial then being tested by the US Navy in the Boeing FB-6 and by Boeing in its new Model 69 fighter.

The composite wood-and-tube fuselage construction used on the Model 40 was changed to an all-steel structure on the Model 40A, pictured here on 24 May 1927.

The lighter 420hp Pratt & Whitney Wasp engine permitted the Model 40A a greater payload, so that the basic design was further altered to include a two-seat cabin in the hope of attracting passenger revenue, in addition to the 1,000lb of mail that could be carried. 3268, the first of the Model 40As, is pictured.

Twenty-four Model 40As were built for the airlines between January and June 1927 (C-286 is pictured). The Model 40A's low operating costs and high revenue-earning potential put the 540A in a class apart and Boeing Air Transport was able to submit the lowest bid for the San Francisco-Chicago route.

Model 40As were converted to Model 40Bs when a new 525hp Pratt & Whitney Hornet engine became available early in 1928. A Model 40C was developed simultaneously, using the Wasp engine but featuring a cabin for four passengers in place of the original two. Ten Model 40Cs were built, nine of them for Pacific Air Transport, which had become part of Boeing Air Transport. The major production series was the Model 40B-4 which combined the Hornet engine of the 40B and the four-place cabin of the 40C. Thirty-nine 40B-4s (including 741K, pictured) were built, and another was delivered to Pratt & Whitney in October 1929 as a flying test-bed for the 650hp R-1860 Hornet engine. Altogether, eighty-two Model 40s were built.

US Navy NB-1 prototype primary trainer (Model 21, A-6749 (518)), powered by a 200hp Lawrence J-1 air-cooled engine. The US Navy tested the first Model 21 extensively and found that it was almost too easy to fly and could not be spun. Changes to make the Model 21 'spinnable' had the opposite effect and the aircraft went into flat spins from which they could not recover!

Starting in December 1924, forty-one NB-1s with 200hp Wright J series engines, and thirty as NB-2 with a war-surplus Wright-Hispano E-4 liquid-cooled engine of 180hp, were delivered to the US Navy. The Model 21 was designed to operate either as a land plane or as a seaplane using a single main float instead of the twin pontoons of the earlier Model Cs. Five Lawrance-engined Model 21s were also delivered to Peru: three in 1924 and two in 1927.

The Model 64, which first flew in February 1926, was designed as an improved land or sea primary trainer to replace the NB and was submitted to the Army as a primary or gunnery trainer. A removable rear cockpit fairing structure permitted rapid change from gun ring to padded headrest.

XN2B-1, one of two Model 81s built in 1927-28 as a development of the Model 64, pictured on 18 May 1928. The XN2B-1 was built for the US Navy and the Model 81A for the Boeing School of Aeronautics. The original Fairchild-Caminez 125hp four-cylinder radial engine was replaced by a more conventional 165hp Wright J-6-5 (R-540) radial in January 1929.

The success of passenger operations with Model 40s on the San Francisco-Chicago route encouraged expansion of the business through the addition of larger aircraft. Four Model 80 trimotor (410hp Pratt & Whitney Wasp) biplanes, which were designed specifically for passenger convenience and comfort, were built with a capacity of twelve passengers, the first being delivered to Boeing Air Transport in August 1928, just two weeks after its first flight.

The Model 80A (793K, the first, pictured) was an improved version, powered by 525hp Pratt & Whitney Hornets, and was capable of carrying eighteen passengers. Ten were built, the first two being delivered with fully cowled engines and the small vertical tail. The large passenger cabins on the Model 80 and 80A were provided with hot and cold running water, forced-air ventilation, leather upholstered seats, and individual reading lamps. The two pilots were enclosed in a roomy cabin ahead of and separate from the passenger cabin.

The eleventh Model 80A (NC233M) was completed as a deluxe executive transport (Model 226) for the Standard Oil Company of California, and the twelfth was constructed as Model 80B with an open cockpit (later converted to 80A-1 with an enclosed cockpit).

The luxurious cabin of the Model 226 executive transport, looking aft. All Model 80s became 80A-1s following service modifications that changed fuel capacity, streamlined engine cowlings, and added more rudder area.

With the Model 80s devoted almost exclusively to Boeing Air Transport's growing passenger service, a need arose for an all mail and cargo plane on the same routes. The first of twenty-five Model 95s, which made its maiden flight on 29 December 1928, were delivered on 18 January 1929. Of those with the traditional open-cockpit configuration (not all pilots liked the enclosed cabin as used on the Model 80) with 89 cubic feet of cargo space, twenty were delivered to Boeing Air Transport, one to National Air Transport, and four to Western Air Express.

Designed initially as a mail- and cargo-carrying plane, the Model 200 Monomail marked a radical new step in aviation when it first appeared on 6 May 1930. It was the first all-metal aircraft of monocoque construction and among its many innovative features was a single, smooth, all-metal low wing of clean cantilever construction, semi-retractable undercarriage, and the use of anti-drag cowlings on the 575hp Pratt & Whitney Hornet B power plants. A second Monomail, with a six-passenger cabin, was built as Model 221. This and the first model (NX-725W, later NC, pictured) were subsequently revised for transcontinental mail and passenger service and were re-designated Model 221A.

The Model 214 (Y1B-9) was a military development that applied the aerodynamic and structural concepts of the Monomail to bomber construction. Traditionally, bombers had until this point been biplane types, mainly of all-wood construction.

Boeing applied the B-9 design concept to the successful Model 247 civil transport whose final design was also influenced by the Monomail. An order for sixty Model 247s was placed while the design was still in the mock-up stage. The type flew on 8 February 1933 and featured retractable landing gear, an enclosed cabin, auto pilot, trim tabs and de-icing equipment, and was powered by two supercharged Pratt & Whitney 550hp S1D1 Wasps (the first time superchargers had been used on a transport type). The original-style ring cowlings, small nacelles and fixed-pitch propellers are evident in this picture of five early Model 247s (NC13348, 13347, and 13328 nearest the camera).

Model 247 cockpit detail showing flight instruments (centre) and the engine and fuel system instruments in front of the co-pilot's control column (right). In 1934 Roscoe Turner and Clyde Pangborn in a 247D came third overall in the Melbourne Centenary Air Race between England and Australia, and second in the transport category.

The 247D (C-73) was an improved version of the original Model 247 and thirteen were built. All US-operated 247s (two were delivered to Deutsche Lufthansa, the German national airline) were subsequently modified to 247D standard with improved Wasp S1H1G engines, full NACA cowlings, controllable-pitch propellers, and sloping windshields. C/n 1726 (pictured), formerly a Model 247, was one of eight 247Ds which served in the Royal Canadian Air Force (with RCAF serial number 7655), before being acquired by Britain and used by the RAF for research into instrument and automatic landing systems.

Here, the RAF roundels and serial number, DZ203, are being sprayed over. Traces of the wartime camouflage can be seen under the new scheme. Apart from the RCAF and RAF, the USAAC also operated twenty-seven 247Ds, between 1942 and 1944, under the military designation C-73.

Boeing, meanwhile, had entered the bomber business, as on 14 April 1934 the Army General Staff issued a request for design proposals for 'Project A', an aircraft capable of carrying a one ton bomb 5,000 miles, to hit targets in Hawaii or Alaska. Boeing proposed the Model 294 (XBLR-1 – experimental bomber, long range), and on 28 June 1934 were awarded a contract for design data, wind tunnel tests and a mock-up. The XBLR-1 (35-277) was re-designated XB-15 by Edmund 'Eddie' T. Allen, test pilot and Director of Aerodynamics and Flight Research, before its first flight on 15 October 1937. (Allen was killed testing the XB-29 on 21 September 1942.) It was at that time the largest aircraft in the world. The XB-15 joined the 2nd BG in August 1938 and set a number of records.

Early in 1936 the beautiful Model 314 was designed to meet a specification issued by Pan-American Airways for a long-range, four-engined flying boat capable of carrying seventy-four passengers and a crew of six to ten. The wing and horizontal tail surfaces of the XB-15, then under construction, were adapted almost intact to meet the requirement. Boeing signed an agreement on 21 July 1936 for six 314s, or 'Clippers' as they were known, and they were all delivered between January and June 1939. Pictured is NC18603 *Yankee Clipper*, operated for the US Navy in the Second World War by PAA.

The first 'Clipper' flew on 7 June 1938 and began on transatlantic airmail service on 20 May 1939, and passenger service on 28 June. Six 314As for PAA with more powerful engines and provision for three extra passengers followed, and the first six 314s were brought up to the same standard. Early in the war, three were purchased by BOAC for operation on the Atlantic route, while three more were acquired by the US Navy and operated by Pan Am crews. NC18602 42-88632 *California Clipper* (pictured) was operated by the US Army in the Second World War. After the war the 'Clippers' were replaced by land plane types.

Work on the Model 300 transport ceased in 1934 when priority was given to the Model 299 bomber, but development was revived three years later in the Model 307, which utilized the wings, nacelles, engines, and original tail surfaces which were standard B-17 components, married to an entirely new fuselage. 42-88627 was one of ten Stratoliners built. The distinctive dorsal fin developed on this model was later used on the B-17E.

In 1937 ten Stratoliners were ordered by US airlines: four PA-307s (S-307) by PAA (including NC19903, pictured above), five SA-307Bs by Transcontinental and Western Air (TWA, now Trans World Airlines), and a single SB-307B by Howard Hughes. The first 307, an S-307 for PAA, flew on 31 December 1938, but was lost on a subsequent test flight. The S-307s remained in Pan Am service until the end of the Second World War but in 1942 all five SA-307Bs were impressed into Army Air Transport Command service as the C-75. In 1944 they were returned to the factory for conversion back to airline standards as SA-307B-1s.

An outstanding feature of the 307, thanks to its circular cross-section, was its first use of cabin pressurization for passenger comfort at sub-stratospheric altitudes. The design also permitted maximum room for thirty-three passengers and five crew, including, for the first time, a flight engineer. After the war the revamped Stratocruisers, now fitted with replacement B-17G components, could carry thirty-eight passengers.

Two
In Pursuit of Perfection

Some 586 aircraft in the P-12/F-4B series were delivered to the Army and the Navy (and a few overseas); the last was on 28 February 1933.

Women workers stitching the upper wing fabric of an MB-3A. In 1921, Boeing was the lowest bidder among six manufacturers competing for an Army contract for 200 Thomas-Morse MB-3A pursuit planes. This was the first sizeable order for new aircraft placed by the military since the Armistice and it provided the company with design experience that saw Boeing become the leading American supplier of single seat pursuit aircraft between 1924 and 1936.

This Thomas-Morse MB-3A pursuit plane came to grief on 7 June 1922.

42

Financed as a private company venture, the first Boeing pursuit, the Model 15 (XPW-9 – Experimental Pursuit, water-cooled design No. 9), flew on 2 June 1923.

Model 15, 23-1217, the second XPW-9 prototype, showing the indented upper wing leading edge and the streamlined cross-axle landing gear of 16-inch cord used on all three examples.

Two FB-2s, modified to operate from aircraft carriers, were designated Boeing Model 53 because of the design changes. Three FB-3s with Packard engines (Model 55) and one FB-4 (Model 54) (pictured, on 15 January 1926) with an experimental Wright 450hp air-cooled P-1 radial were delivered for test. Twin wooden floats were fitted and after delivery the Navy converted the FB-4 to FB-6 by changing the P-1 engine for a Pratt & Whitney Wasp radial.

The Navy ordered twenty-seven production FB-5s (Model 67) powered with the 520hp Packard 2A-1500. The first flew on 7 October 1926.

Women workers covering the fuselage of an FB-5 with fabric, 13 January 1927. All twenty-seven FB-5s were delivered on 21 January 1927, being ferried by barges directly to the carrier *Langley* in Seattle harbour.

Assembly of mail planes, and PW-9C pursuits (left). Production experience with the MB-3As and careful study of the newest aerodynamic and structural concepts convinced Boeing engineers that they could produce a better pursuit plane than anything then available. The principal source of dissatisfaction with the MB-3A was the wooden fuselage. Welded steel tubing had been used successfully during the First World War. The gas welding process with hand torches had disadvantages, so Boeing developed an arc welding process. The new fuselage construction was so successful that the Army gave Boeing additional DH-4 modification contracts that called for replacement of the original wooden fuselages with steel.

Altogether, 123 PW-9s (including 25-301, pictured) were delivered, ending with the PW-9D (Model 16D) of 1928.

The XP-7 (Model 93, pictured) was the last PW-9D, which was re-designated when fitted temporarily with a new 600hp Curtiss V-1570 engine.

The US Navy ordered sixteen PW-9s for shore-based duties with the Marine Corps but only ten (including A-6893, pictured) were delivered, in December 1925, under the Naval designation of FB-1, for Fighter, Boeing. Nine of these served with the USMC Expeditionary Force in China in June 1928.

The F2B-1 was a direct development of the PW-9/FB series, designed to use the 425hp Pratt & Whitney Wasp engine designed by the Navy in the FB-6. In addition to the prototype XF2B-1, the Navy bought thirty-two production F2B-1s for use on aircraft carriers.

The XF3B-1 which flew on 2 March 1927 was offered as an improved fighter version of the F2B-1 with new, larger wings, but it was only when it re-emerged as a fighter-bomber (Model 77) that it was taken up by the Navy. A contract for seventy-three F3B-1s, each with a P&W R-1340 Wasp engine, followed.

The three F-2B-1s of the Sea Hawks, the US Navy's first precision aerobatic team, performing their characteristic tied-together aerobatics. The team would take off, manoeuvre and land with their wing tips joined by 50ft lengths of rope, which had streamers attached to improve visibility from the ground. Eventually a whole squadron of F-2Bs was able to fly and land tied together!

Early in 1928 all of Boeing's fighter plane experience culminated in two new prototype pursuits, the Model 83 (Navy XF4B-1 No. 1), which first flew on 25 June 1928, and the Model 89 (Navy XF4B-1 No. 2, pictured carrying a 500lb bomb under its belly), which flew on 7 August. The F4B was a dual-purpose design, as both fighter and dive bomber.

The first XF4B-1 was reworked to production configuration (A8129, pictured on 17 June 1929) and delivered to the Navy as the second article on the F4B-1 (Model 99) contract. Following the XFF4B-1 tests, the Navy ordered twenty-seven production F4B-1s (A-8130/8156), and the Army ordered nine identical P-12s (Model 102) and one as XP-12A (Model 101).

Wooden wings, bolted aluminium tube fuselage, and corrugated control surfaces of the P-12 are evident in this uncovered view.

P-12 29-353 *Pan American*, the first Army Model 102 built, was turned over to Captain Ira C. Eaker on 26 February 1929, shortly after his famous 150-hour endurance flight.

In 1929 ninety examples of the Model 102B (P-12B; 29-333 is pictured) were ordered, the largest single Army order for fighters since 1921. The optional 55-gallon auxiliary fuel tank is fitted under the belly.

AAC 29-329, the first P-12B, was modified by the AAC as XP-12G to test turbo-superchargers and ring cowlings and was fitted with a three-bladed prop to absorb the additional power, before reverting to P-12B.

The last twenty-five P-12Es were completed as P-12Fs (Model 251), while 32-42 (pictured) became the P-12J when it was used at Wright Field to test a supercharged Pratt & Whitney SR-1340H engine and a special bomb sight. Later it became a YP-12K to test the SR-1340E fuel-injected engine, before reverting to P-12E.

P-12F (32-101), the twenty-fifth and last of the production run, was fitted with an experimental enclosed cockpit canopy and is pictured on 11 May 1932, six days before delivery.

Four commercial and export derivatives were developed as Model 100s and a special two-seat 100A was built. NX872H (pictured) was sold to Pratt & Whitney for use as a flying test bed.

Model 218 (XP-925, 925A) X-66W was a Boeing-owned aeroplane used to test new features for the P-12/F-4B series and first flew on 29 September 1930. It was sold to China after US testing and, flown by American volunteer pilot Robert Short, is reported to have destroyed two out of three attacking Japanese fighters before being shot down over Shanghai in 1932.

The Model 227 (P-12D, XP-12H) resulted from slightly modifying the last thirty-five of the original 131 aircraft in the P-12C order. Deliveries began on 25 February 1931 and finished on 28 April.

The thirty-third P-12D (31-273) was re-designated XP-12H when the AAC fitted it with an experimental geared Pratt & Whitney GISR-1340E engine but this proved unsatisfactory and the plane was reconverted to a P-12D in June 1932.

F4B-2 (Model 223) 8635 of VF-6B (later, VF-3) with the famous 'Felix the Cat' with a bomb in his claws. The US Navy ordered forty-six F4B-2s and the first was delivered on 2 January 1931, the last on 2 May.

On 3 March 1931, the AAC ordered 135 P-12Es (Model 234) (32-44 pictured). The enlarged 'Panama' headrest contains a life raft.

P-12E (Model 234) pictured on 19 September 1931.

P-12E (Model 234) 32-47 in AAC livery, pictured on 29 May 1934.

The US Navy followed with an order on 23 April 1931 for 113 similar Model 235s, twenty-one of them as F4B-3s. The F4Bs were first delivered to the Marine Corps VF-9M (East Coast), and were soon followed by delivery to VF-10M (West Coast) in late 1932. Pictured are three of VB-10M Bombing Squadron 4's F4B-3s in 1933 after the squadron's changeover from Fighting Squadron 10.

In addition, ninety-two Model 235s, like this VF-5 (Fighting Squadron 5) machine, were ordered as F4B-4s, which had larger vertical tail surfaces.

Fourteen of the original F4B-4s were diverted from the US Navy order and modified slightly for delivery to Brazil (called *1932* – Model 256) as land-based fighters between 14 September and 9 October 1932.

Five Model 203 primary trainers, powered by 150hp Axelson engines (the third with the original small tail and Axelson engine is pictured on 25 October 1929), were built for the Boeing School of Aeronautics. All were converted to the 203A type by installation of 165hp Wright J-6-5 Whirlwind engines.

Two additional Model 203s were built by students at the school. They were later converted to 203As with the change to the Wright engine: NC12748 in 1935 and NC13392, pictured, in 1936. Three 203As were converted to 203B advanced trainers with 220hp Lycoming engines.

With the biplane fighter era almost at an end in 1930, Boeing submitted Models 202 (XP-15) (pictured), and 205 (XF5B-1), almost identical all-metal monoplane versions of the established P-12/F-4B, to the AAC and US Navy. While neither was ordered into production, the new semi-monocoque fuselage structure was used on later versions of the P-12/F-4B.

The Model 236 (XF6B-1) was developed as a possible successor to the F4B-4, but the era of the classic biplane fighter with fixed landing gear was over and the type did not enter production.

Boeing's Model 248, which first flew on 20 March 1932, was the first all-metal monoplane fighter. Boeing built three prototypes (XP-936 pictured) at its own expense but the Army loaned Pratt & Whitney 522hp SR-1340E Wasp engines, instruments, and military equipment for the project, which was carefully co-ordinated with the Army to ensure that its requirements were met.

The third XP936, which went to Selfridge Field, Michigan, where it was tested by the Army. During service tests the XP-26s became Y1P-26 and finally plain P-26. After testing, the Army purchased the XP926s as XP-26 on 15 June 1932.

P-26A pictured on 16 December 1933. A total of 111 P-26As were ordered by the AAC. Their top speed was 222mph, 27mph faster than the P-12F, but at 30,700ft they fell 800ft short of the biplane's absolute ceiling.

Twelve export versions, eleven for China and one for Spain, were built as Model 281. Lt José Kare, in one of nine P-26As turned over to the Philippine Army late in 1941, shot down a Japanese Zero fighter during their attack on the Philippines. Here, Captain Jesus Villamor enters his P-26 fighter during a December 1941 alert. This photograph was present in many Philippine homes during the Japanese occupation.

Boeing cleaned up the P-36 design by adopting cantilever wing construction to remove the need for a wire-braced wing, and fitted a retractable undercarriage. Two models were developed simultaneously for the AAC and the US Navy, the former being designated YP-29, formerly the XP-940 (Model 264, pictured on 17 January 1934). In March the XP-940 was returned to the factory for modification and became the YP-29A.

The XF7B-1 (Model 273, pictured on 14 September 1933), similar to the XP-940, first flew in September 1933. It was the first low-wing monoplane fighter tested by the Navy.

The second Model 264, designated YP-29 because of the purchase contract having been signed following testing of the XP-940, was completed with a large and roomy glasshouse enclosure around the cockpit.

The original cockpit enclosure of the XP-940 was replaced by an open cockpit and a redesigned headrest and the aircraft became YP-29A (pictured) when purchased by the Army. Although 16mph faster than the P-26A, the YP-29A's greater weight restricted manoeuvrability and its service ceiling, and the intended P-29A production order never materialized.

Three
Big Ass Birds

B-17 Flying Fortresses silhouetted against the sun at altitude over Germany.

X13372, the Model 299, shown here at its roll out at Boeing Field, Seattle, 17 July 1935 when, because its wingspan was greater than the width of the hangar door, it had to be rolled out sideways on wheeled dollies. The Model 299 was flown for the first time on 28 July by the company test pilot, Leslie Tower.

The clean lines of the Model 299 owed much to the sleek Model 247 airliner which was scaled up into the much bigger Model 299 by using many of the engineering innovations that had been developed on the earlier Model 294 (XB-15) project.

Testing was almost complete and the Air Corps about to confer the title XB-17 to the Model 299 when, on 30 October 1935, the aircraft crashed with Major Ployer P. 'Pete' Hill (chief of Wright Field's Flight Testing Section) at the controls. Hill died later that day and Leslie Tower, Boeing test pilot, died a few days later. The subsequent investigation concluded that the crash was a result of the mechanical ground locks not having been unlocked prior to take off.

Ill-luck also dogged the Y1B-17 service test machine development. The first Y1B-17, 36-149, was rolled out on 30 September 1936 and it flew for the first time on 2 December, but on the 7th it nosed over during landing. However, the thirteen service test Y1B-17s went into service with the 2nd BG, at Langley Field, Virginia, from March to August 1937, and were flown 1.8 million miles over land and sea without a problem. Six of the Y1B-17s which made the goodwill flight to Buenos Aires, Argentina, in February 1938, are pictured over New York City. They covered a total of 12,000 miles without serious incident. The Fortress's place in history was assured.

The hoped-for large production contracts for the B-17B (Model 299E, later Model 299M) were slow in coming. A requirement for ten B-17Bs had been received on 3 August 1937 and by 30 June 1938 orders stood at just thirty-nine. Problems with the superchargers, which tended to fail very frequently, meant that the first B-17B (38-211) did not fly until 27 June 1939. The first B-17Bs were delivered to the AAC between October 1939 and 30 March 1940. In 1940-41 many B-17Bs were revamped and fitted with new devices such as flush-type waist windows for .50 calibre guns.

Fortuitously for Boeing, on 18 May 1940 the company received a very timely contract from the French Government for 240 DB-7B (A-20C) attack bombers. When completed, the fall of France meant that these (including AL399, pictured) were delivered to England as Boston IIIs. Some were diverted to Russia. Night fighter conversions became Havocs. A further 140 A-20Cs were constructed for the USAAC.

Meanwhile, the Boeing Canada plant at Vancouver, British Columbia, which had produced Blackburn Shark III torpedo planes for the RCAF in 1938 and 1939, was expanded to undertake aircraft repair and conversion. Also produced were fifty-five Consolidated PBY-5A Canso amphibians for the RCAF and 307 PBY-5 and -6 Catalina flying boats under the US Navy designation of PB2B-1 (pictured) and PB2B-2 for the US Navy and British Empire services.

Only eighteen B-17Cs (Model 299H) were ordered, on 10 August 1939, for the AAC and it was not until April 1940 that the Army finally exercised its option for forty-two more. Meanwhile, twenty Model 299U/B-17Cs (Fortress Is) were ordered by Britain for the RAF from the 1939 contract. The B-17C first flew on 21 July 1940.

Fortress I (40-2064), which became AN528 'B-Baker' in No. 90 Squadron RAF, pictured during an early test flight. (At first, the Fortress Is for the RAF had 'AM' serial letters applied in error but they were changed later to 'AN'.) RAF Forts first went to war on 8 July 1941, when three bombed Wilhelmshafen. 'B-Baker' had joined 90 Squadron on 4 June but caught fire running up her engines at dispersal at Polebrook on 3 July and was burnt out.

Forty-two B-17Cs, which had been ordered on 17 April 1940, required so many modifications, mostly due to combat experience in Europe by the RAF, that, on 9 September 1940, they were redesignated as B-17Ds. More armour plate was added and armament doubled in the ventral 'bathtub' and upper positions, while additional sockets were added for the .30 calibre nose gun, making seven guns in all. Self-sealing fuel tanks were installed and the bomb release system was redesigned.

Finally, on 12 July 1940, Boeing was advised by the War Department that orders for 512 more B-17s would be raised, but material shortages delayed production of the B-17E and the example did not make its maiden flight until 5 September 1941, four months behind schedule. Boeing received orders for 812 B-17Es but after 512 had been built, the remaining 300 aircraft were converted to B-17F production.

B-17Es 41-2459 and 41-2461 at Shallufa, Egypt, en route to join the 19th BG in Java. The 19th fought a brave but losing battle in the Philippines after the Japanese invasion. 41-2459 and 41-2461 were first used in action on 16 January 1942. Lt J.L. 'Duke' Du Frane's and Maj. C.F. Necrasson's respective crews had to force land at Kendari, Borneo, and were strafed by Zeros. Du Frane's B-17 was disabled but his crew escaped and were later evacuated to Java. The aircraft was later blown up during the US retreat.

B-17E 41-2435 of the 40th BS, 19th BG, pictured over the Owen Stanleys, was shot down off Buna on 12 August 1942. Note the power-operated Bendix belly gun turret, which was installed in the first 112 Es on the production line, and was fired by a gunner lying prone and facing aft, sighting the guns through a periscope arrangement of angled mirrors.

B-17E 41-2600 *Esmerelda* with the much improved ball turret, designed by Sperry, which finally replaced the cumbersome Bendix installation.

B-17F-1-BO 41-24344 from the first block of F models. The BVD pool was created when Boeing agreed to let Lockheed-Vega and Douglas Aircraft build the B-17F under licence. The first B-17F was delivered to the AAF on 30 May 1942. 41-24344 was assigned to the 326th BS, 92nd BG, at Bovingdon in 1942, and joined the 414th BS, 97th BG, at Polebrook in August. It was lost on the group's last mission from England on 21 October 1942, along with Capt. John M. Bennett's crew.

B-17F-55-BO 42-29467 pictured on 18 December 1942. Named *Flak Dodger*, this aircraft flew in the MTO, initially with the 348th BS, 99th BG. The 'F' looked similar to the B-17E, save for a frameless Plexiglas nose, but no fewer than 400 changes and modifications were made, most of them being carried out on the production line itself.

In theatre the olive drab, and later natural metal, factory finish B-17s were nearly always applied with 'nose art' (usually the naked female form) and the practice became synonymous with 8th and 15th Air Force B-17 combat crews. The Fortress earned many sobriquets, namely, 'queen of the skies' and, universally, 'the big ass bird'.

'Flak thick enough to walk on' went the saying, and is evident here in August 1943. At Schweinfurt and Regensburg on 17 August 1943, the 8th Air Force lost sixty B-17s shot down and twenty-seven so badly damaged that they never flew again. Another sixty, which continued to North African bases after the bombing, had to be left behind for repair. The second big Schweinfurt raid, 14 October 1943, cost the 8th another sixty B-17s, plus 138 damaged.

B-17F-70-BO 42-29815 LG-P, *Miami Clipper* (left), and B-17F-65-BO 42-29656 *Terrible Ten*, LG-S, in the 322nd BS, 91st BG, 8th Air Force, under attack by a Bf 110 on 22 January 1944. On 20 February 42-29656, which originally had been assigned to the 358th BS, 303rd BG, and called *Skunkface*, failed to return with 2/Lt Ernest B. Kidd's crew. Two men were killed and eight were captured. *Miami Clipper*, which had first been assigned to the 367th BS, 306th BG, was scrapped at Walnut Ridge, Arkansas, January 1946.

SNAFU – 'Situation Normal, All Fouled Up', although the acronym was known differently in some circles! This particular SNAFU is B-17G-15-BO 42-31393 in the 388th BG, 8th AF, which, renamed *Snaky*, failed to return with 2/Lt Donald E. Walker's crew on 29 April 1944.

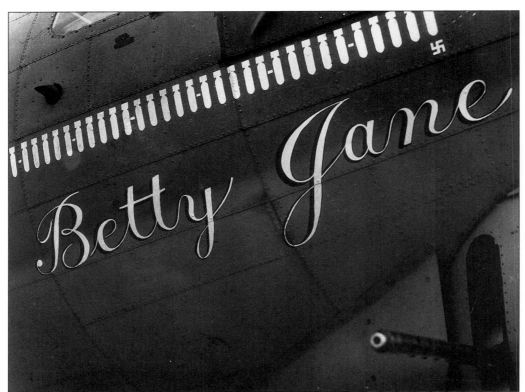

B-17G-35-BO 42-32027 *Betty Jane* in the 427th BS, 303rd BG, failed to return with 2/Lt C.W. Heleen's crew on 13 September 1944. Eight of the crew were captured.

'Any landing you can walk away from is a good landing.' This B-17 made it back to England – just.

B-17G-1-BO 42-31032 (which was assigned to the 422nd Night Leaflet Squadron, 305th BG, on 25 November 1943) from the first production block. During September 1943, the B-17G (Model 299-O), which first flew on 21 May, appeared in Europe. Its most significant feature was a 'chin turret', fitted for forward defence.

B-17G-20-BO 42-31454 BO-B *St Anthony* in the 368th BS, 306th BG, with B-17G-1-BO 42-31065 GY-Z in the 367th BS, and four other B-17s, in formation. *St Anthony* joined the 100th BG at Thorpe Abbotts in April 1945 and then the ATC on 24 May, being lost on 31 January 1946.

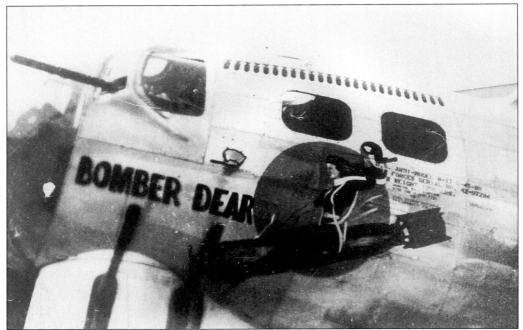

B-17G-45-BO 42-97234 LG-M *Bomber Dear* in the 322nd BS, 91st BG, went missing in action with Lt Donald R. Sparkman's crew on 2 November 1944.

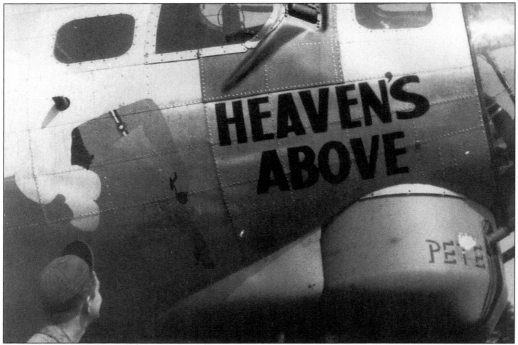

B-17G-45-BO 42-97328 *Heaven's Above* in the 561st BS, 388th BG, 3rd Bomb Division, 8th AF, at Knettishall, Suffolk. The electrically driven Bendix Model 'D' chin turret is enclosed in a movable aluminium alloy housing containing two .50 calibre M-2 machine guns.

B-17G-70-BO 43-37675, VE-N, originally called *Trudie's Terror*, in the 532nd BS, 381st BG, in formation with two 535th BS B-17Gs. On 1 March 1945 43-37675, now called *Patches 'N' Prayers*, force-landed in France, was repaired and saw out the rest of the war, being scrapped at Kingman, Arizona, in December 1945.

Hollywood movie star Clark Gable, who flew a few missions with the 8th AF, is pictured at the fighter station at Bodney, Norfolk, in 1943, in front of B-17G-75-BO 42-29835 *Pistol Ball* in the 511th BS, 351st BG, after flying in from Polebrook where the actor was making a gunnery training film for the USAF.

Young men came from every state in America to man the B-17s. This is Robert L. Miller's crew, pictured during training in the US before they joined the 493rd BG at Debach, Suffolk, and flew their personally named B-17G, *Sonof A Blitz*.

B-17G-75-BO 43-37883 *Blue Streak* in the 834th BS, 486th BG, flown by 2/Lt David Paris, hurtles down after taking a direct flak hit in the left main fuel tank over Merseburg on 2 November 1944. All nine crew were killed in action.

B-17F-100-BO 42-30359 QJ-D in the 339th BS, 96th BG, pictured in North Africa after the Regensburg shuttle bombing mission, 17 August 1943. This aircraft was lost with 2/Lt Linwood D. Langley's crew on 29 November 1943.

B-17F-100-BO 42-30366 BX-A, *Fertile Myrtle III* in the 338th BS, 96th BG at Snetterton Heath. It crashed at Silver Fox Farm, Taverham, Norwich, on 16 December 1943.

B-17F-110-BO 42-30607 *Pat Hand* of the 337th BS, 96th BG, 8th AF, flown by 2/Lt Kenneth E. Murphy, takes a flak hit over Paris during a raid on the air park at Romilly-sur-Seine on 15 September 1943. One man survived and nine crew died.

B-17G 43-37993 *Mah Ideel*, which served in the 401st and 324th BSs, 91st BG, at Bassingbourn before returning to the USA to be scrapped at Kingman, Arizona, in December 1945. Bert Stiles, author of *Serenade to The Big Bird*, is standing at the centre.

'Where Angels Fear To Tread'. High in the stratosphere B-17s in the 452nd BG, 8th AF, etch their give-away contrails in the sky. B-17G-40-BO 42-97069/M *Mon Tete Rouge II* (bottom left) failed to return on 4 December 1944 with 2/Lt Lawrence Downy Jnr's crew.

In Italy, B-17s equipped six bomb groups in the 5th Bomb Wing. B-17G-55-DL 44-6606 of the 2nd BG piloted by Lt Notheis, landed at Miskolc airfield, Hungary, on 21 January 1945 after being damaged during a raid on Vienna. Rumanian ground crews fixed an Hs 129 main wheel to the Fortress to act as a tail wheel to enable the B-17 to take off again!

German fighter pilot's eye view of a B-17. Despite their formidable armament, once a Fort had fallen out of formation, they were usually easy prey for Focke Wulf 190s and Bf 109s.

The RAF operated late model B-17s in Coastal Command and as RCM aircraft in 100 Group (pictured) for 'spoofing' and radar-jamming operations.

Fortress II (B-17F-40-BO 42-52349, (pictured on a test flight in the US in 1942) arrived in the UK in December 1942 and, coded FA707, served with 206 and 220 Squadrons of RAF Coastal Command, being lost in a crash in the Azores on 26 July 1944.

Fortress III HB-788 (B-17G-50-BO 42-102439) joined No. 214 Squadron, 100 Group RAF at Oulton, Norfolk, where it was coded BU-B, and was lost on 7 November 1944.

B-17G-40-BO 42-97130 in the 731st BS, 452nd BG, 8th AF.

B-17G-70-BO 43-37716 *Five Grand*, the 5,000th B-17 built at Boeing Seattle since Pearl Harbor, was covered with the signatures of Boeing employees. *Five Grand* flew seventy missions in the 96th BG at Snetterton Heath, England, and was scrapped, like thousands of others, at Kingman, Arizona, in 1945.

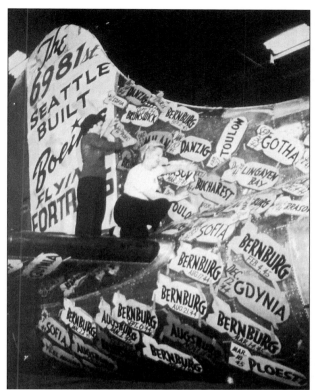

Boeing ceased Fortress production on 13 April 1945 to concentrate on the B-29 Superfortress. 43-39508, from Block B-17G-110-BO, was the 6,981st Fortress built by Boeing and is decorated with removeable paper bomb cut-outs commemorating enemy targets bombed by B-17s.

B-17E 41-9210 was put on display at the University of Minnesota in November 1945 for seven years. After operating in Canada and Florida, the B-17 was purchased by Compañía Boliviana de Aviación of La Paz in July 1964 and registered CP-753. On 3 January 1974, operating now with Frigorificos Reyes, the port undercarriage collapsed while taxiing. In 1992 the B-17 (N8WJ) was acquired by Scott D. Smith of Colorado Springs.

B-17G-90-BO 43-38635 was used after the war by the Atomic Energy Commission. In 1959 it was registered N3702G before being converted to a fire-tanker (No. 61) in 1960. In 1979 it was restored, named *Virgin's Delight*, and put on display at the Castle Air Museum, Castle AFB, Merced, California. The original *Virgin's Delight* was flown by Col. (later Brig. Gen.) Frederick Castle (after whom the base is named), who was killed in action on 24 December 1944. He was posthumously awarded the Medal of Honor.

Three experimental Model 400 single-seat fighter-torpedo bombers, powered by a 2,500hp P&W R-4360 driving a six-blade contra-rotating airscrew, were built for the US Navy as the XF8B-1. The first aircraft (pictured) flew on 27 November 1944.

Cessna Aircraft of Wichita, Kansas, was selected to build 750 Waco CG-4A troop carrying gliders but the company sub-contracted the entire order to the Wichita Division of Boeing, who literally built them in the aisles of the new Plant 2 while tooling up for Superfortress production.

B-29s on the ramps outside Seattle Plant 2 late in the war. Early in 1942 the plant was concealed with a camouflage hill, complete with city housing, streets, and cars.

Superfortresses never served operationally in England in the Second World War, although YB-29 41-36963, one of a batch of fourteen Wichita-built service test aircraft, seen here at Horsham St Faith, Norwich, did a tour of USAAF bases in East Anglia to make the Germans believe that perhaps they just might be used.

The XPBB-1 (Model 344) using a wing similar to the B-29, was built to a US Navy requirement for a very long range flying boat patrol-bomber. In 1942 the need for this type of seaplane diminished so the Renton factory, built for the production of the PBB-1 'Sea Ranger' for the US Navy, was turned over to the Army for production of the B-29 Superfortress.

B-29A-BN 42-93844, with both sets of bomb bay doors open. Renton-built aircraft differed only in having four guns instead of two in the front turret.

B-29s in the 500th VHBG, 73rd Bomb Wing, dropping bombs on Japan.

B-29 *Censored* in the 39th VHBG taxies out at North Field, Guam. The 39th flew their first mission to Maug, in the northern Marianas, early in April 1945.

YKB-29J-MO (RB-29J) 44-86398, one of 116 B-29s converted to KB-29P tanker aircraft at Renton in 1950-51, refuelling a Republic F-84G Thunderjet by means of the 'Flying Boom' developed by Boeing to replace the hose refuelling system.

A US Navy P2B-1S, one of four B-29-BWs obtained in 1947, which was used to air-launch the rocket-powered Douglas D-558-II research aircraft.

In March 1948 two B-29s demonstrated the feasibility of air-to-air refuelling using trailing hoses and grappling hooks to make contact. A total of ninety-two B-29s were re-designated KB-29Ms, and six were used to refuel the B-50A *Lucky Lady II*, which made the first ever non-stop round-the-world flight in February 1949. During the time of the Korean War in 1950-53, B-29s equipped four wings and one reconnaissance squadron in SAC, and the 19th BG in the 20th AF.

Britain obtained eighty-eight ex-mothballed B-29s and B-29As, calling them Washington B.Is, on loan from the US, between 1950 and 1955, to supplement RAF Bomber Command's ageing Lincolns, pending delivery of Canberra and V-bomber jet aircraft. Here, B-29A-BN 44-61599 is pictured on arrival at RAF Marham, Norfolk, in March 1950 where No. 149 Squadron became the first to be equipped with the Washington B.I.

Senior RAF officers salute the arrival of four Washingtons. In all, Washingtons equipped eight front-line squadrons in Bomber Command, and by 1958 almost all of the 'stop-gap' bombers had been returned to the US.

The Pratt & Whitney Wasp Major-engined B-29D was re-designated the B-50A before service deliveries took place; the first B-50A (46-002) flew on 25 June 1947. The taller fin and rudder, which were among several new features and improvements, are evident in this picture of B-50A 46-026.

47-122, one of fourteen RB-50B (RB-50E) reconnaissance versions of the B-50A which were modified at Wichita.

Some 112 of the 136 B-50As and B-50Bs that had been converted to KB-50 hose tankers by Hayes Industries were designated KB-50J. Here KB-50J 48-123 refuels three North American F-100A Super Sabres of Tactical Air Command simultaneously.

Four
Stratocracy

Shades of *Doctor Strangelove*.

Model 367-5-5 YC-97A 45-59590, one of ten service test models of the C-97 Stratofreighter of the Air Transport Command, crossing San Francisco's Golden Gate bridge. The C-97 was designed in 1942 as a heavy cargo transport and bore the same aerodynamic and structural relationship to the B-29 that the Model 307 Stratoliner bore to the B-17. The first YC-97A flew on 28 January 1948 and the first of fifty production C-97As for the Military Air Transport service flew in June 1949.

The Model 377 Stratocruiser was an airline development of the C-97 and fifty-six were built side-by-side with B-50s on the Seattle production lines between 1947 and 1949. Pan American World Airways were the largest Stratocruiser operator, with twenty-nine, including Model 377-110-26 N1023V, pictured here.

Model 377-10-26 N1030V *Clipper Southern Cross* of Pan American World Airways. Ten PAA - 26s were modified to Super Stratocruisers by adding an additional 450 gallons of fuel to permit non-stop flights between New York and London and Paris.

Stratocruisers offered the last word in passenger comfort and between fifty-five and a hundred people could be accommodated according to the length of the route and type of service. A complete galley for hot meal service was located near the tail. Men's and women's washrooms separated the forward compartments from the main passenger cabin, where a spiral stairway led to a deck lounge on the lower deck behind the wing. When fitted out as a sleeper aircraft (pictured), the 377 was equipped with twenty-eight upper and lower berth units plus five seats.

Korean war casualties on board a Military Air Transport Service (MATS) MC-97C bound for the US. Fourteen C-97Cs were built.

A stunning night shot of BOAC Stratocruisers at Heathrow. The nearest aircraft is G-ALSA *Cathay*, one of six 377-10-28s bought by the airline. Altogether, BOAC acquired seventeen Stratocruisers (four later operated with SAS), and in 1958 Transocean Airlines of Oakland, California, bought thirteen of these.

Model 377-10-32 G-AKGH *Caledonia* of BOAC, one of six -32s ordered by the airline, and one of the ten Stratocruisers sold to Transocean Airlines of Oakland, California, in 1958, to make way for newer jet transports.

C-97A 49-2591, one of three from a total of fifty built which were converted to KC-97A configuration, seen here refuelling a Boeing B-50D 49-304. Outwardly, the C-97A differed from the YC-97A in the installation of a chin radome housing AN/APS-42 search radar.

Nine Stratocruisers have been converted to 'Guppy' aircraft. N1024V, the second PAA 377-10-26, was converted to a 377-PG (Pregnant Guppy) to transport large spacecraft sections and flew for the first time on 16 September 1962. This was followed by five Super Guppies (377-SG/Model 201), and three Mini Guppies (377-MG/Model 101). Airbus Industrie in Toulouse, France, uses four Super Guppies, (pictured in April 1990) for airlifting major Airbus components around Europe.

The L-15 Scout (Wichita Model 200/Seattle Model 451) liaison aircraft was designed and built in Wichita. Two XL-15s and ten YL-15s were completed in 1947-48, the first flight being made on 13 July 1947.

Boeing development of a jet bomber began in 1943 and the Model 450 was approved in April 1946. 46-065, seen here being rolled out on 12 September 1947, was the first of the two XB-47 prototypes to fly from Boeing Field, Seattle, to nearby Moses Lake AFB, on 17 December 1947.

The first B-47A flew on 25 June 1950. 49-1909, the last of ten Wichita-built Model 450-10-9 B-47As, fitted with eighteen external solid-fuel JATO (jet-assisted take-off) rockets, each having a thrust of 1,000lb. Altogether, 2,032 B-47s were built; 1,373 by Boeing, 274 Es by Douglas, and 385 E-LMs by Lockheed.

B-47D 51-2103, one of two (the other was 51-2046) which became XB-47Ds when converted to act as test beds for the Wright YT-49-W-1 turboprop engine.

The designation B-52 was originally assigned in 1946 to a straight-wing long-range bomber to be powered by six turboprop engines. By October 1948 the design had undergone a rapid transformation with swept wings, and eight Pratt & Whitney J57 turbo jets, and the new B-52 Stratofortress was designed and built as Boeing Model 464. Pictured is YB-52 49-231, the second prototype, which first flew on 15 March 1952. The XB-52 (49-230) flew for the first time on 2 October 1952.

B-52B 53-394 in flight. Thirty B-52Bs and seventeen RB-52Bs were built. The RB-52B carried a photo-reconnaissance or ECM capsule complete with operating personnel which could be installed in the bomb bay for specialized missions. Deliveries to SAC began on 29 June 1955, to the 93rd Heavy Bomb Wing at Castle AFB, California. On 21 May 1956 a B-52B dropped the first airborne hydrogen bomb from 50,000ft above Bikini Atoll.

On 18 January 1957 three B-52Bs of the 93rd Heavy Bomb Wing completed a two-day non-stop flight around the world in 45hr 19min, refuelling three times en route from KC-97s, at an average speed of 520mph for the 24,325 miles.

B-52C 54-2669 in flight. A total of thirty-five were built, with 3,000-gallon auxiliary fuel tanks. The first flew on 9 March 1956. This was the first B-52 model to use the white thermal reflecting paint on the under surfaces.

A Wichita-built B-52D, its wheels lowered to slow down to the lower speed of the propeller-driven KC-97, moves in to begin refuelling. A total of sixty-nine Model 464-201-7 (B-52D)s were built at Wichita, and 101 B-52Ds were produced at Seattle.

Tall tails. B-52E 56-635 being refuelled by a KC-135 aerial tanker. Forty-two Model 464-259 B-52Es were built at Seattle and fifty-eight at Wichita. The first B-52E flew on 3 October 1957. A total of ninety-nine B-52Fs were produced at Seattle and Wichita, with the latter plant also building 193 B-52Gs and 102 B-52Hs.

Short-finned B-52G 57-6471 in flight. This model (464-253) first flew on 26 October 1958 and 193 were built at Wichita. The G could carry two AGM-28 (formerly GAM-77) Hound Dog stand-off missiles, one on a pylon under each wing between the inboard nacelles and the fuselage. These were phased out in the 1970s, to be replaced by the AGM-69. (The white cross on black square is a photo-theodolite target.)

B-52G 57-6518 with AGM-69 subsonic Short Range Attack Missiles (SRAM). Up to twenty could be carried, six on a pylon under each wing and eight on a rotary launcher in the bomb bay, with the capability of hitting several targets hundreds of miles apart on one mission. In 1982-83 the SRAMs were supplemented by a new subsonic Air Launched Cruise Missile (ALCM), twelve of which could be carried on the B-52G and B-52H.

The Vertol Aircraft Corporation at Morton, Pennsylvania, was acquired in 1960 and it became the Boeing Vertol Division, before changing to the Boeing Vertol Co. in 1972. Among its first production designs was the CH-46A 'Sea Knight' (a special version of the twenty-five-passenger Vertol 107-11), which has been ordered by the USMC, US Navy (UH-46A) and several overseas air forces.

The first of the UH-61 Chinook
helicopters was delivered in 1967
and it has become the primary
transport helicopter for the US
Army and several air forces
overseas. The first flight for the
RAF's HC Mk 1 Chinook was on
23 March 1980 at Boeing Vertol's
suburban Philadelphia plant.

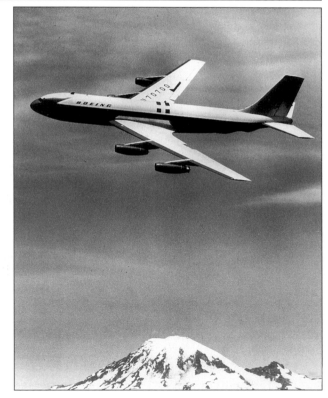

In August 1952 Boeing
announced plans to invest $16
million to build an entirely new
jet-powered transport, the Model
707. The prototype carried the
designation 367-80 which Boeing
technicians called the 'Dash
Eighty'. The 367-80 707
(N70700) (pictured) flew on 15
July 1954.

Sabena 707-329 OO-SJN, one of ten 707-300s bought by the Belgian world airline from Boeing.

707-3B5C HL-7406 of Korean Airlines, the only 707 series model used by this airline.

By 1988 some 120 military 707 variants of various designations, like this Luftwaffe 707-307C (one of four built new and procured by the USAF under the designation C-137 in 1968) had been received by Boeing.

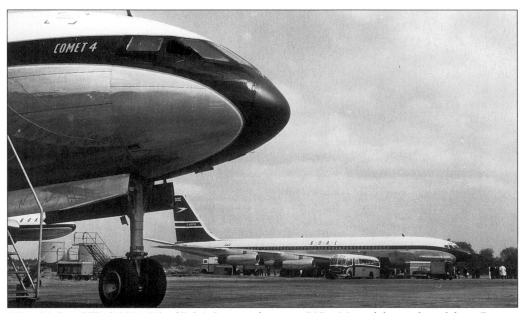

707-436 G-APFD (N5091K) of BOAC, one of sixteen 707-436 models purchased from Boeing by the British airline.

Contracts for the Model 727-100 short-to-medium-range jet, to replace the many piston and turboprop aircraft in service, were signed in December 1960. The first 727, designated 727-22 (N7001U, for United Airlines), was rolled out at Renton on 27 November 1962. Some 408 727-100s were built.

N7001U pictured on its first flight, 9 February 1963.

Model 727-100 N72700 (No. 1), temporarily registered N1784B, in flight. Model 727 production finally reached 1,831 aircraft through -100, -100C, and -200 aircraft.

No 727s were sold to the US Armed Forces, but retired airline models were acquired in 1983-84. This 21 Squadron, 15 Wing, Belgian Air Force 727QC (CB-02) based at Melsbroek is pictured taxiing in at Moi International Airport, Mombasa, Kenya, during the international relief effort in February 1993. The last 727 was delivered in September 1984.

Model 727 A9C-BA belonging to Al Bahrain undergoing a 'stretch' at Marshalls of Cambridge. The length was increased by adding 10ft fuselage plugs ahead of and behind the wing to increase passenger seating to 189. The first flight of the stretched 727 (727-200) took place on 27 July 1967.

The prototype Model 737-100 (N73700) first flew on 9 April 1967 and the first of 1,095 737-200s was delivered on 29 December. Lufthansa was the initial customer for the 737-100 with twenty-two ordered (only thirty 737-100s were built).

737-200 G-BICV belonging to Dan-Air. The -200 series was powered by Pratt & Whitney JT8D-9A engines of 15,500lb thrust. The thrust reversers were replaced by a new target type, which added a 45-inch extension to the rear of the nacelles. A total of 1,097 737-200s were built.

The 737 is the charter airlines' dream machine. Dan-Air operated two 737-300s. Pictured at Gatwick on the occasion of the type's first commercial flight with the airline is G-BNNJ. The -300 entered production in March 1981.

737-300 G-SCUH of Dan-Air in flight. The -300, which was first delivered on 28 November 1984, differs from previous models in having Pratt & Whitney CFM-56 engines with 'flat-bottomed' nacelles (to permit ground clearance) in place of the JT8Ds of the -100 and -200 series.

Under a $81.7 million contract, nineteen T-43A Airborne Navigator trainers, based on the basic Model 737 airliner, were produced for the USAF Training Command in 1973-74 to replace part of its fleet of T-29s.

Early in 1966 Pan Am placed a conditional order for twenty-five of the first of Boeing's giant jetliners, the Model 747, capable of carrying 363-490 passengers, or 125 tons of cargo. Full-scale production began in 1967 in a plant measuring 200 million cubic feet on a 780-acre site adjoining Paine Field near Everett, where the first 747-100 (N7470, pictured) was rolled out on 30 September 1968. N7470 flew for the first time on 9 February 1969, and deliveries of 747-121 production models to Pan Am began on 13 December that year.

The first 747-100-121, Pan-Am's *Clipper Constitution*, arriving at London Heathrow on 12 January 1970, three hours late from New York after one of its Pratt & Whitney JT9D fan-jet engines gave trouble and had to be changed. The aircraft carried over 300 employees of Pan-American, the company which was to introduce the jumbo jet on non-stop passenger flights from New York to London on 21 January 1970.

VC-137C 62-6000 was the first of two special 707-353Bs ordered in 1961 for the Office of the President of the United States, and was delivered in October 1962. The second (72-7000) was delivered in August 1972 and was used until replacement by Boeing 747s (C-25A).

President John F. Kennedy is greeted after disembarking from VC-137C 62-6000 at the start of an official visit to RAF Waddington, Lincolnshire, on 29 June 1963.

KC-135A (717-146) 0-10317 landing at RAF Gan on 9 March 1972. The Model 367-80 was a logical outgrowth of the basic 707 airliner design and the first 29 KC-135As were given the company designation 717-100A. Note the circumferential stiffeners (aluminium strips) applied to the rear fuselage in front of the dorsal fin, devised to prevent the impingement of turbojet sound waves causing sonic fatigue in the aluminium skin of the rear fuselage.

KC-135A 63-8036 refuelling KC-135B 62-3581. The tanker was ordered into limited production in July 1954 and first flew on 31 August 1956. Deliveries to SAC began on 28 June 1957 and when the final delivery was made in January 1965, 820 had been built by Boeing-Renton.

RC-135B 61-4845, one of the last 30 C-135As, powered by Pratt & Whitney TF33-P-5 turbofans, and one of ten used as photographic and electronic reconnaissance aircraft.

KC-135A 60-356 of MATS, one of four converted to RC-135D in 1962-63.

C-135B 61-331 of MATS, one of thirty built. Five C-135Bs were converted to VC-135Bs and ten were converted to WC-135Bs.

Interior view of an EC-135 Airborne Command Post. A SAC general officer and a highly skilled team of controllers and operations specialists are always on board.

In 1972 the USAF invited manufacturers to propose potential replacements for the Lockheed C-130 Hercules. Boeing responded with the YC-14 STOL (Short Take Off and Landing) transport, powered by two 55,000lb thrust GE turbofans mounted on the wing. Two YC-14s were built (72-1873 and 1874) but no production orders were placed. The project is now under scrutiny once more.

E-3A 73-1676, the first of three Advanced Airborne Command Posts, which first flew on 19 June 1973 and which was delivered to the USAF on 16 July. The E-3As were later converted to E-4B configuration.

The first E-4B built as such, with the added Super High Frequency radio housing on the fuselage. First flown 23 April 1975 and delivered to the USAF less than fully equipped on 4 August 1976, the aircraft was redelivered on 21 December 1979.

EC-137D 71-1407, one of two civil 707-320Bs in 1963 (71-1408 being the other) which were modified to serve as prototypes for a new military Airborne Warning and Control System (AWACS) with the addition of a Westinghouse AN/APY-1 radar system and large external radome. The two 707-137Ds were delivered in 1972 and redelivered as E-3As in USAF light grey/white colouring in 1977-78. Beginning in March 1977, thirty-two additional E-3A Sentries were purchased by the USAF for AWACS operations. Eighteen were later purchased by NATO, five by Saudi Arabia and four by France.

747-238BL VH-EBA of Quantas Australian Airlines, which operated a fleet of two combis and twenty-two 747-200s, the first seventeen 747Bs powered by Pratt & Whitney engines, the rest being fitted with RB.211 power plants.

747s nearing completion at Seattle in 1989. They will be moved across the highway bridge nearby at night (so as not to distract drivers), for painting in their respective airline liveries.

On 18 February 1977 747-123 N905NA (ex-N9668), the NASA Shuttle Carrier (pictured in June 1983 carrying *Enterprise* from the Paris Air Show to Stansted) made its first flight carrying the unmanned shuttle.

The first Model 757-200 (N757A) designated 757-225, fitted with Rolls-Royce RB.211 engines, flew for the first time on 19 February 1982.

First deliveries of the 757 began in December 1982 (Model 757-2T7 G-MONE of Monarch Airlines at Luton Airport, pictured, in 1984). Within six years, 368 757-200s were on order.

Boeing 767 prototype, designated 767-200 (N767BA), which was rolled out at Everett on 4 August 1981 and which flew for the first time on 26 September that year. Within seven years 316 767-200s and -300s were on order.

The 747 marked its twentieth anniversary on 30 September 1988 when the first built, followed by the newest model, the -400, (the 735th 747 built), flew in close formation over Seattle, Washington.

The 400-passenger 747-400 and 146-passenger 737-400, the newest additions to the Boeing family of jet airliners, also flew in formation over the north western United States in September 1988.

Seven Boeing E-3A AWACS aircraft were purchased by Britain in 1991 and all were refurbished by Marshall of Cambridge (pictured). The first flight of the first E-3D Sentry for the RAF (ZH101) took place at Seattle on 5 January 1990.

RAF E-3D Sentry ZH106 in flight with a Tornado F3. At Waddington four are in service with No. 8 Squadron, and three with No. 23 Squadron.